ALL the Doors to HOLLYWOOD and HOW to OPEN Them

ANNE M. STRICK

All the *Doors* to Hollywood and HOW to *Open* Them

Copyright © 2011 Anne M. Strick
All rights reserved.
ISBN: 1477569154
ISBN-13: 9781477569153

Represented by:
Michael Hamilburg Mitchell Hamilurg Agency
Los Angeles 90049
California
E-mail:Mhamilburg@aol.com
Ph.:310-471-4024

ANNE M. STRICK

CONTENTS

Acknowledgments	v
Introduction	1
Accountant/Book Keeper	3
Production designer	7
Art Director	11
Construction Coordinator	15
Gaffer	23
Grip	27
Props	31
Scenic Artist	35
Special Effects	41
Transportation	45

All the *Doors* to Hollywood and HOW to *Open* Them

Graphic Design	**49**
Set Decorator	**53**
Costume Designer	**57**
Make-Up	**61**
Publicist	**65**
Postscript	**71**
Chart of IATSE Guilds and Locals for Further Information, Contact and Employment Opportunities	**72**
Other Books by Anne M. Strick	**77**

ACKOWLEDGMENTS

My first thanks go first to those seventeen persons who, in the following pages, generously gave me their time, thought, information and enthusiasm – sharing their years of working experience and adventure. Obviously, this handbook would not exist without them!

My thanks go also to Jeremiah Samuels, Executive Producer on *The Conspirator* and *Brothers* among others, who began his own career as a Production Assistant on commercial productions. Out of the wealth of his own working background and overflowing Rolodex, he directed me to the rewarding people in this book.

And finally, my appreciation to the man who in another way made this book possible: my computer magician Ramis Sadrieh, of Technology For You, who over the course of six books almost always arrived within twenty-four hours of my sad pleas for help, and whose skill, patience and humor are notable; particularly considering the frequency and oddities of my computer dramas.

To all the foregoing, my continuing gratitude.

Anne M. Strick

In China for movie 'Tai-Pan'

In rainforest in Cameroon, West Africa, for movie 'Greystoke'

On set in London with actor in ape costume as Tarzan's mother

In rainforest in Cameroon, West Africa, for movie 'Greystoke'

On set in London with actor in ape costume as Tarzan's mother

ALL THE DOORS TO HOLLYWOOD & HOW TO OPEN THEM

Some time ago, I needed a job. I had spent six years finishing a book, living on and finally totally depleting my savings. At last, I found employment with a start-up corporate public relations firm, worked there for six months, was fired for insubordination, refused several apologetic hire-back offers, and was on the scramble again. But in those six months, I had learned the publicity game. Several friends suggested I try the movie business. I put together a resumé, and on my third interview, was hired as publicist for the movie **The Border** with Jack Nicholson. The fun began.

Most of us - perhaps you - have an almost insatiable interest in all things Hollywood. Often we fantasize - secretly, perhaps - about being part of the film business ourselves. But being so seems impossible.

What actors and stars do, what producers and directors and writers do, seems light-years beyond our reach - despite all the advice books telling us how to make the rareified leap. We lack, we believe, the talents, the training, the connections, the youth and physical perfection, the long grinding grit and sheer gumption necessary to break in. Even, possibly, the luck.

But we have other abilities. Abilities rarely associated with film-making, but ones that stand behind the screen and make the magic possible. Abilities without which there could be no movies at all. The high-profile professions, so excessively publicized, so glamorous and brightly lit, are not the only doors to Hollywood. There are other doors - many doors - doors we walk through, without a thought, every day - to professions absolutely necessary to the Hollywood show's going on.

This book tells you what those other doors are.

On these doors, most of us - ordinary people in every city - nurses, carpenters, teachers, first-aid workers, journalists, electricians, photo lab and metal workers, secretaries, sketch artists, plasterers, makeup artists, cooks, hairdressers, model-makers, truck drivers, photographers, seamstresses, accountants, and so many more - need only knock. We will, of course, probably have to knock more than once, as for any job. Nor is ultimate employment inevitable – as for any job.

But if the doors open, we will be extremely well-paid. We will take great pride in our skills and enjoy the camaraderie of our colleagues. We will be delighted with our union benefits. And we will have, for all of our lives, wonderful behind-the-scenes stories to tell.

These are some of the doors; this is how some people have opened them. And these are some of the adventures they've had.

Perhaps you'll do the same. I did.

ACCOUNTANT/BOOK KEEPER

What does a bookkeeper or accountant do on a movie?

"Essentially", says Accountant MICHAEL MENZIES - veteran of such movies as **Conan The Destroyer, Body of Evidence** and **Tai-Pan** - "my job is to work with the film's producer and the studio to create the budget. And then simply help them stick to it".

Once the movie's funding is finalized and production begins, the accountant meets with the producer each week and reports on the movie's financial status: which departments threaten to exceed their allotted budgets, and which, remaining under budget, might balance the overage. Also important is estimating the "one day cost" - the cost of going each day over the total budget - which helps the producer make decisions as to which scenes must perhaps be cut, which departments must find cost-saving tricks, or which may splurge a bit more.

All the *Doors* to Hollywood and HOW to *Open* Them

How did you find the first job? What was your training?
"I had no book keeping or accounting training at all. Absolutely none." New Zealand-born, Menzies began as a free-lance magazine writer in London, became an administrator at the New Zealand Consulate in New York, and happened to meet the great choreographer Agnes De Mille, for whom he produced an Emmy-nominated documentary - which brought him the offer of a job as Financial Administrator for Orion Films. "The job was pretty simple - I just had to keep an eye on the production manager and the accountant". From there he was offered a job by producer Dino De Laurentiis as Production Accountant on the movie **Amityville Two.** "And that's what I've been, ever since."

What do you enjoy about the work?
"The people, the travel - China, Mexico, Hong Kong, Bratislava –. And there've been so many funny moments", Menzies says. "Like watching Arnold Schwarzenegger straining to squeeze his bulk into a miniscule VW cab in Mexico City – and trying to pull a buddy in with him! 'Hey Arnold'", Menzies called, "you could EAT that cab!" On **Conan The Destroyer,** he watched Arnold and Wilt Chamberlain take gag photos with the movie's publicist.

"She was about 5'2", and she was glaring up at seven foot four inch Wilt – she came about up to his belly button – shaking her finger, supposedly protecting Arnold, who was pretending to cower behind her – both guys in full **Conan** costume."

On **Sky Captain and The World of Tomorrow,** producer Raffaella De Laurentiis discovered that neither

Gwyneth Paltrow nor Jude Law had a clue about her legendary Italian film-star mother, Silvana Mangano. "So Raffaella plunked them down with my assistant, Eduardo, and here the two leads sat, like two school kids, open-mouthed, while she gave them a film history lesson for an hour!"

Gwyneth Paltrow nor Jude Law had a clue about her legendary Italian film-star mother, Silvana Mangano. "So Raffaella plunked them down with my assistant, Eduardo, and here the two leads sat, like two school kids, open-mouthed, while she gave them a film history lesson for an hour!"

PRODUCTION DESIGNER

What does a Production Designer actually do? How do you go about it?

"I'm the point person for the movie's overall look", says Production Designer BILL BRZESKI. "Anywhere from helping pick locations, reflecting time of day, overseeing all the real to virtual scenery and the shape of buildings, to designing an entire world". The title of Production Designer, he says, originated with the movie **Gone with the Wind.** "Before then, films often had more than one Art Director, and it became custom to name a Supervising Art Director. With William Mendes, on GWTW, that designation became Production Designer."

In movies' early days, he tells, most Art Directors came from the world of architecture. "They had to design schools, buildings, cities". And conversely, some of early Los Angeles architecture was influenced by the fancies of movies the architects worked on -

"castles, witches' cottages, Moorish palaces, world-of-future stuff.".

After you've signed on for a job, how do you proceed?
"Before I've been hired, I've of course discussed concept with the director, so that he or she knows we're in synch. When I have the job, the first thing I do is break the script down and design the concept – the look, the visual feel, suggested locations. I'll do a presentation – more or less elaborate, depending on the size of the film and the budget – sketches, photos perhaps, models. And then get the director's take on all of it. Make whatever changes we come up with. Of course I've already begun to hire – Art Department, location scouts, Decorator. I talk with Accounting, and make whatever changes the budget requires. Feedback is a critical part of the whole process."

How did you begin?
"Since I was eighteen", Bill says, "I knew I was going to work in theatre design. In high school, I was into music and band, and worked on the musicals we did every year. So as an undergrad at Miami University, I began as a music major – but really struggled at it. In my freshman year, I discovered the scene shop next to the band rooms, and volunteered to work on a play. I was hooked – and changed my major within a week."

Brzeski went on to New York University, where he studied theatre, and got a Masters in Arts. "In the '80's, I moved to Los Angeles, and began to find work in television - moving from variety shows to sitcoms, and finally to features. My first assistant design job was on a show –

still running in Las Vegas – called **Jubilee**. My first job as production designer was in 1986 on **Growing Pains** for Warner Brothers. I did over 800 television episodes of multi-camera sitcoms from **Ellen** to **The Nanny**. I was constantly reinventing myself".

Bill's first big screen movie was **Matilda,** in 1996, which launched him into feature films. It was directed by Danny Devito, with Rhea Perlman and Mara Wilson. "The previous Designer had been fired. A friend called and said 'Come on in for an interview'. I got the job, but it was three weeks before the start of principal photography, there was no design concept on any piece of paper, and not a single person in the art department. It had disaster written all over it. But I kept it together and got through it with great success. Actually, I think it was some of my best design."

Who are some of the actors and directors you've worked with?
"There've been so many terrific ones - Jack Nicholson, in **As Good as It Gets** and **Bucket List,** Morgan Freeman, Shirley McClaine, Baryshnikov, Danny DeVito, Rob Reiner – I could go on."

Where've you gone on location?
"All over. Asia, Canada, Thailand, China, Hong Kong – as well as Nashville, Atlanta, Chicago, Portland –."

Any location stories?
"This one comes under the heading of 'Never underestimate the importance of food on location!' On **The Forbidden Kingdom** in China, we had a food crisis. We were shooting in a rural area and the food was bad. I

mean very *bad*. We began to get depressed and bicker about almost everything. At which point our Italian painter announced that some ingredients for a pasta dinner had just arrived for him from Rome. Well – he made Carbonara for five of us. The meal was amazing – there we were, grown men, actually crying. Now when I go on location, I work on the food thing from Day One!!!"

What is the work like? What do you enjoy about it? Your favorite film?

"It's a little like the military. A strict hierarchy – everyone has a very specific job and does absolutely nothing else. And you operate with strict loyalty to the director. It's sort of focusing on a very large task with one idea. What I like is that you get to do your thing really quickly – generally three to six months time – but what you do lives on. And you get to design your fantasies. One of the rewards is that more people get to see your work than that of other designers – we have such influence on people and they don't even know it. As to a favorite film - I guess one of my favorites was **The Forbidden Kingdom,** in China. It opened me up to traveling in China, and the possibilities of Asia in general. It was a great adventure! I think the bottom line is – find a way to do something you love!"

ART DIRECTOR

Just what does an Art Director do?

"It's a multi-faceted job", says MARK GARNER. "I'm kind of an office manager at first, putting the Art Department together. The film's concept, its mood and look, is determined by the Director and Production Designer – and I create drawings to illustrate the concept. I supervise the Construction Coordinator, Set Designer and Set Decorator to carry it out - the Set Designer is essentially a draftsman in set construction. At the same time, everything is coordinated with the production assistants and the Assistant Art Director. Likewise with the Location Manager. The locations have to be practical as well as appropriate. And I create the budget for all of it, in line with the movie's overall budget – and see that we stick to it!"

What was your training for all of this?

Garner began with a degree in architecture and landscape architecture. Working in landscape, he was feeling dissatisfied, when he got an offer of a job on a small HBO feature, **Someone Has to Shoot the Pictures**, as a Set Designer. Another HBO film followed – and then came his first big screen movie, **My Girl,** with Mcauley Culkin, Jamie Lee Curtis and Dan Akroyd.

"I had to learn the language of set design – what 'wild walls' were, for instance – walls made to be removed easily to allow camera maneuvers - and how to draw for sets that would be torn down, instead of the real thing."

His second feature as Set Designer was **Wilder Napalm,** with Deborah Winger and Dennis Quaid. "The assistant Art Director, Ross Gallichotte, was my mentor. I also Art Directed a few short-lived, low budget TV series and maintain today that if you can do that successfully you could run a small country!"

Where have you worked?

"All over the country. Texas, Ohio, Kentucky, Rhode Island, which is where we shot **Dan in Real Life** with Steve Carell - my first Art Director credit on a feature film. And Savannah, the location for Robert Redford's **Conspirator,** with Robin Wright and Kevin Kline, was fabulous – rich in history. And I love historical films. One that I'm particularly proud of is HBO's **From the Earth to the Moon.** That was a series of thirteen two hour movies, set in the '50's and '60's, about the space race - a big part of our national history. We shot in Florida, of course."

What do you enjoy about what you do?

"Many things. I love the opportunity to go to places, like Cape Canaveral, restricted to everyone else. I love having shaken the hands of men who've walked on the moon. I love that we work with people who influence the world in many ways - fashion, and in design. I love seeing our drawings given life on film. We have so many perks – of places, of people – every job is different."

"And I come from a small rural town on the west coast of Florida. I'm the first in my family to finish college. I was raised largely on a farm and - coming from that background - my life seems a series of incredible adventures."

CONSTRUCTION COORDINATOR

What does a Construction Coordinator do?

"I'm the general contractor for the scenery", says TOM MORRIS. "I put together the team of craftsmen to get all of the sets built – Carpenters – 'Propmakers' in the film industry - Welders, Painters, Sculptors, Plasterers, Greensmen and Laborers. The size of the team can be anywhere from 20 people to 200 or more, depending on the size of the film, the scope and character of the sets, and the time allowed to complete them. We work for the Art Department, which tells us which scenes will be completely constructed on the sound stage, which shot on location and what alterations must be done to those locations. In short, Construction is responsible for the entire physical environment of the film, even the vegetable garden in which the heroine may pick tomatoes!"

What was your background? How did you get your first job in the business?

"I've been at this ever since the 8th grade in Asheville, North Carolina! Literally. The class did a play I wrote, about Valley Forge, in which I played George Washington – but I did a lot of backstage stuff too – helped build scenery, props. Then I majored in drama In college - acting again and working backstage - and did repertory during summers. After graduation I got a job as an apprentice carpenter for the Spoleto Festival. The following season I became a staff carpenter, and then head Flyman at the opera house – the Flyman is the one who raises and lowers scenery, and the curtain. Then for a time I ran the Scene Shop, where scenery is made.

One day a friend told me that a movie crew was in town and were looking for someone to build scenery. The movie was **Heart of Midnight**, with Jennifer Jason Leigh, Peter Coyote, and Sly Stallone's brother Frank Stallone. He said they paid well – 'thirteen or fourteen'! I thought he meant thirteen or fourteen dollars an hour, and that sounded darn good. So I interviewed. Turned out it was thirteen or fourteen thousand a week! I was terrified - wondering what I had gotten myself into and what was going to be expected of me for so much money!

But after the first day, I realized that the job was just what I had been doing since the 8th grade – building scenery. Since I was the one in charge of the crew, it turned out that, on my first film, I was the Construction Coordinator, though I'd never heard that term before."

Where have you worked?

"Fourteen or so States, New Mexico to Massachusetts. And foreign places like Puerto Rico, Ecuador, the Bahamas, the Dominican Republic."

Some of your favorite stories?

In 2000, Tom was working in Quito, Ecuador, on **Proof of Life,** with Russell Crowe and Meg Ryan. "Our largely Spanish-speaking crew numbered between 80 and 200, along with 10 experienced film construction people from the U.S. We lived and worked above 10,000 feet, which took a little getting used to at first."

There were unique challenges on the show, "one of which involved lowering the water level of a lake that was located above 15,000 feet in a place called *Papallacta.*" The film company had shot a few scenes on the shore of the lake earlier in the schedule. A couple of months later, they decided that they needed to shoot some additional scenes there, but when the location scout went back up to *Papallacta,* he discovered that the water level of the lake had risen and that the set was now under water. "We had to pump a lot of water out of the lake, working 24 hours a day for several days, to re-expose the set to match the earlier footage."

Additionally, they had to build two and a half miles of road up the side of a mountain. "We laid lots of material down on the road, and lots of material washed right back down again. It was Ecuador's rainy season – which is pretty darn rainy! But we had to persist - the set was scheduled to be shot, and the road had to be finished. The crew worked through the nights in pitch dark – there's not much light that high, and away from civilization. We discovered that diesel engines don't work so well at that altitude, not to mention or own lungs!"

Luckily the production had a first-rate local crew. Everyone worked in the rain, all day, every day. "We had a tent in which the crew ate and we catered hot meals for them - plus candy in the afternoon. At the same time, we had to build the set at the end of the road, without having a real road to get there. But we couldn't delay that either. So we used Ecuadorian Army helicopters to ferry the materials up to the location. At the same time, we had to keep the road in constant repair, maintain it day and night against the constant rain. So one night, Russell Crowe decided to skip the hour's drive back to town and sleep on the set in his trailer. Well – around three a.m. he was awakened by very loud diesel-powered thumping noises – to his dismay, the huge steam-roller we used to pack the gravel was compacting away right by his quarters. I guess it wasn't as restful a night as he thought it might have been!"

At a different location, a bridge had to be built over a gorge at the base of a waterfall called *El Pailón del Diablo* - the Devil's Cauldron. "The only access to this location was a forty-five minute hike down into the gorge. When we started, it was still the rainy season and cloudy most of the day. But when the clouds finally cleared a month or so later, we saw that we were working at the base of *Tunguragua,* a twenty-thousand foot active volcano."

For MGM, Tom worked on **Into the Blue,** which was shot in the Bahamas. A lot of the film took place under water, because in the story, a plane has crashed and sunk.

"So we not only sank one plane – we sank three DC-3s, into which we had to build scenery for different story stages - all in fifty feet of water, and on the edge of both a coral reef and an abrupt three thousand foot deep ocean trench! We had to be intensely careful - not to contaminate the delicate reef, not to let the planes tumble into the trench - and to keep them steady for shooting – all in the winter ocean. In addition, we built a shipwrecked Spanish Galleon we carried out on a salvage ship and lowered into the water. The problem was, despite being partially filled with concrete, the galleon floated. So we had to lift it back on board and add quite a bit of steel flat bar to make it stay down on the bottom. But I've got to say - it was a gorgeous set when we finished!"

On the same show, Tom was also asked to build a number of the props, including cocaine bricks to be stashed in the plane. "These last had to be manufactured with a very specific density so that they would be neutrally buoyant - remain at the depth for which they'd been intended. A final irony, Tom recalls, "was that the bricks refused to obey! One of the carpenters, a woman with a chemistry degree who does wonders with plastics and molds, solved it. We called her fondly our Props Tart."

This all sounds daunting. How do you begin?
"At the start of a show, we get a script, a shooting schedule, and the designs from the Art Department. From these, I have to determine what each craft needs to do for each set, how long it will take them, and when they need to begin. Everything has to be done in a certain order by the different crafts, and completed in time to allow Set Decoration time to dress the set and Grip/

Set Lighting time to pre-rig the set, and sometimes time for the actors to rehearse on the set.

In an ideal world each craft would start and finish their work before the next craft would begin. But given the time constraints on most films, that's not what generally happens. More often the crafts have to work side by side and sometimes almost on top of each other. So sometimes, we have to call for crews at night due to overlapping needs for the same space.

I also oversee Trans Lights - that's the giant backing with an image printed on it – an indoors scene, or a nighttime scene – sort of a giant transparency. If you light it from the front, it's day. From the back, it's night. I see that the Greenman puts flowers, or weeds - or maybe a scattering of dried leaves - where he should. Plants can tell you a lot about a scene – whether it's cared for or neglected. Or a sapling between the rails of a train track will show it's long unused."

Any other responsibilities?

"Two main ones", Tom explains: Budgeting/tracking and scheduling. "I'm responsible - with the Art Department - for submitting and managing the budget for all aspects of the construction of the sets. And then I'm kind of an engineer. Although I'm not actually accredited, I still have to construct things that hold up, and are approved by a real engineer. When one of them tells me 'You're not a bad engineer', I'm happy!"

What do you enjoy about the work?

"Every show is different, every set is different, every day is different. You end up working in so many different places, beautiful and not-so-beautiful. At times, it's like being a tourist on someone else's dime. It's creative and collaborative. I enjoy being part of the team that makes so many disparate parts and watching different people come together to create something that didn't exist before and will only exist on film when we're done. Every show starts and then finishes - that exact team has only come together for that one film. The next one will be different from the last. So I'd say that the most important aspect of my job is putting together the right team for the film. And if there's something you don't like, it'll end!"

GAFFER

What is a Gaffer? What does a Gaffer do?

A Gaffer, JAY YOWLER tells us, is head of the electrical department and right hand man to the Director of Photography (who is sometimes referred to as the Lighting Cameraman). "The D.P., by the way, is really the most important person on the set. Any D.P. can be a director, but not every director can be a D.P. – and I've worked with a lot of them!"

The Gaffer and the Key Grip, Jay explains, work hand in hand: The Grip is responsible, at the Gaffer's direction, for cutting light or diffusing it as the D.P. wants, for increasing or darkening it, for hanging perhaps twenty or thirty lights in different places and different heights. All to help create the mood that the Director and the D.P. want. "Light is critical to mood."

"Then", Jay says, "you have to balance your lighting in relation to ambient light, which changes throughout the day. And there's different lighting for different sorts of movies – comedies are bright and flat, dramas want more contrast. It takes a lot of hands to do all this – my crew will range from five to perhaps twenty people. And then I have a Best Boy who is sort of my foreman and handles all the paper work – and he has his own crew of four or five electricians, too."

What was your background for all of this?
"I've been in the business since I was twenty. My best friend was from a seven-generation circus family in Wilmington, North Carolina. I hung around them, and my first job was as an unpaid apprentice, aiming at working my way up. I started by helping build generators, then learned how to operate them – and gradually knew more and more. I started gaffing when I was twenty-four – my first paid job was building a generator!" And his first movie, at Dino De Laurentiis' Wilmington Studio, was on the film **Maximum Overdrive** – as a driver!

Where does the term "Gaffer" come from?
"It comes from England. In the era of gas lights, before electric lights on streets, a gas lighter used to go around at dusk with a pole called a 'gaff' to light the lamps. So he was called a gaffer. And the term translated to the lighting of electric lamps on sets."

Where have you worked?
"Just about all over the country, in every state – as well as Puerto Rico, the Bahamas, Mexico, Canada, and Russia."

What have been some of your favorite movie jobs?

"I've done so many I can't count - **Blonde Ambition, A Nightmare On Elm Street, Fame** – but I think the Farrelly Brothers films are among my best experiences. I'm referring to **Something about Mary, Dumb and Dumber, King Pin, Osmosis Jones, Say It Ain't So, Me, Myself and Irene.** Peter and Bobby Farrelly make it just a lot of fun to be on the set."

Who've been among your favorite actors?

"Again, so many. Bill Murray comes to mind and Charlton Heston – extremely courteous and professional and helpful. If for instance their stand-ins were off set for a moment, they'd volunteer to stand in for themselves. And Sally Field – she'd just sit there knitting, never leave the set, always thoughtful."

Do any particular film adventures come to mind?

"Well, there was **The Darkest Hour** in Moscow. The toughest film I ever did. It was a Sci-Fi movie, a six-month shoot, and an all-Russian crew. They were hard workers, but not of the skill level I was used to, and the equipment wasn't up to snuff. We had translators, but too often what they passed on to the crew wasn't what I'd said. I didn't have a good dimmer board operator, to program the lights – it's an essential job, and hard to find a really first-rate one. Thought we'd never wrap. A nightmare."

And then, Jay recalls, there was Michael Mann's movie **Manhunter.** "There were three days left of shooting, and I'd just climbed on top of the generator – when suddenly I heard three 'bangs!' and three bullets, real live bullets, went whizzing right past my head. I leaped off the genie, and the Transportation Captain appeared in a special effects truck and I jumped in and then there were more shots -. Terrifying. It turned out that the director ordered real bullets so as to increase the 'reality' of the film! No apologies at his end. I swore I'd never work with him again!"

What do you enjoy about the work?
"It's always different. You respond to new challenges, you get to light anything, anywhere. And you meet and work with so many talented, creative people. You exchange ideas. You get to travel, experience new places. I couldn't do office work, a nine to five – this is the job that suits me perfectly!"

GRIP

What is a Grip? What does a Grip do?

"Grips are sort of like the Sea Bees of the film crew", says ART BARTELS, among whose movies are **Ocean's Eleven** with Matt Damon and **Along Came Polly**, with Jennifer Aniston and Ben Stiller.

"We're the production's physical support system. If the cameraman says, 'We need a light up there', we figure out a way to hang it. Or if a too-blue sky is the problem, we find out how wide the shot will be, what kind of lens the camera will use, and then tent the appropriate area with black. We help the producer keep within the budget, help the director carry out his or her vision - we have to know photography and light and geography.

We scout locations with the Director, the Producer and the Photographer, and advise them what's possible within the projected budget. 'This location will work, this one won't.' We figure out the geography of a shot, in terms of the light wanted. If morning sun is the aim and we're shooting at midday, we just cover a whole street with silk fabric to soften the light, make it more flattering. And in locations like Hawaii, or Jamaica, we do that a lot! We keep an eye on safety issues, too. The Key Grip - the lead Grip - is the set's safety officer. If the First Assistant Director doesn't spot a particular danger, we point it out."

How big a crew do you generally have?

"It varies with the budget and the nature of the script. The average crew includes the Key Grip – me – the Best Boy, Dolly Grip and four company Grips. The Best Boy directs the others, makes sure all materials are in stock and in place, and handles the office work."

How did you get started?

"I knocked on a lot of doors. I'd worked in a photo lab, processing stills, I'd worked in small theatre, helping with the lighting and set construction - but when a guy walked up my driveway to repossess my car, I thought it was time to make some real money. I was twenty-one or twenty-two years old. I thought I'd combine my photo, theatre, and construction experience and try to break into movies. My first job was in film commercials. Within two years I had a house in Malibu and drove a company car. My first feature film was **Four Friends**, directed by Arthur Penn."

What do you like about the work?

"Just about everything. I've worked with some impressive people. After we finished shooting **Polly**, in Hawaii, my wife and I decided to stay on for a week's vacation. When I went to pay the bill - about three hundred and fifty to four hundred a night - I was told Ben Stiller had already covered it - and was handed a note from him thanking me for all my help! You don't forget something like that.

And then there's shooting the breeze with people like Matt Damon, who always wanted to talk baseball, and fascinating people like Jane Fonda and Levon Helm, the drummer from Bob Dylan's band. And remarkable 'Old Hollywood' actors - like Maureen O'Hara and Anthony Quinn. Their professionalism was amazing. They never left the set because they were so engaged in talking with the crew - they asked questions, they told us stories, told how things used to be done –.

With the old Westerns, for instance, the roads in places like Monument Valley were too bad to drive in and out of locations each day, so everyone slept there in tents, with one big Club House tent for socializing, and games. O'Hara is seventy-eight years old now, and sits on the set until one a.m., and doesn't look tired, and is still beautiful – what a woman!"

What else do you enjoy?
"Each movie is sort of a new family. For three or four intense months, we eat together six days a week, sleep in the same hotels, enjoy the same parties, and share the same dramas. And often in great places - Costa Rica, Hawaii, Jamaica.

And I'm always learning and inventing. For instance - how to use whatever materials are locally available, how to make bamboo and wire do for wood and nails and plastic supports - thanks to the locals, who do things like that all the time. I'm never bored - it's great!"

PROPS

What is Props' job?

"Well", says Prop Master PETER BANKINS, among whose movies is **Monster's Ball,** shot in part in Louisiana State Prison, "we're responsible for everything the actors handle. Newspapers, watches and jewelry, maps, sports equipment, police equipment, cell phones, computers, weapons, paintings the actors may pretend to work on - all of it."

How did you get started?

"I was about twenty-five years old. I'd worked as an extra on a couple of films - **Blackula, Coogan's Bluff** - and then as a production assistant on television commercials - but I began to pay attention to a friend who did props. And I thought 'I can do that!'

Another friend, Michael Milgrom, was a Property Master doing television commercials in Hollywood. He helped me get a job as a go-fer production assistant.

All the *Doors* to Hollywood and HOW to *Open* Them

After a few months as a jack-of-all-trades, I began working as a property assistant, on Pepsi, McDonalds and Dubonnet Wine commercials.

In those days, there was a union called Nabet – National Association of Film Broadcasters and Technicians - and in it, unlike today's IATSE, it was easy to move up in grade quickly. Today, you have to have worked ten thousand hours as an assistant before you qualify to take the requisite entry test. Back then you just took the test. So I passed the test, and the union set me up on my first job as full-fledged Property Master on a Johnson's Wax commercial. Other jobs followed, and I gradually built up a reputation.

I met others, including Ed Markley, also a friend of Michael Milgrom – and we three had in common all being immigrant boys from Eastern Europe. Ed was the Unit Manager on my first two jobs, and he recommended me to Irby Smith, the producer on my first movie of any note, **Young Guns.** That film, and subsequent ones with Smith, such as **Major League, Young Guns Two, Rookie of The Year,** helped propel my career."

Have you traveled a lot?

"You name it. Lisbon, Montreal, Genoa, Egypt - all along the Nile, Luxor and Carnhac - Panama, Acapulco, Amsterdam, Africa, the French Riviera –."

What actors have you particularly enjoyed?

"So many. Jack Lemon, George C. Scott, Will Ferrell, Billy Bob Thornton, Ben Kingsley, Jennifer Connelly, Nicole Kidman, Gene Hackman –. And Barbara Streisand, Julia Roberts, Annette Bening, Hallie Berry, Emilio Estevez –. All the women were really sweet.

And I especially enjoyed working with David Mamet, the writer-director. I worked on three of his films, **Heist**, **Spartan** with Val Kilmer, and **Red Belt**."

What in particular did you enjoy about about Mamet?
"The great thing about working with David is that he's a very upbeat guy. He's very appreciative of everyone's efforts and even when he makes changes, he does it with good grace. I can't tell you how many times he's come up to me and said 'Peter, I've got a DFI for you' – DFI stands for Different Fucking Idea. Somehow, working with David, you feel your job is very meaningful."

Can you give us a Mamet story?
"Well, on **Spartan** there was a gun fight scheduled first thing in the morning. I arrived at work to discover that on the location move the night before, a heavy cart had knocked the combination lock off the gun safe, and I couldn't open it. I told David what had happened, and called a locksmith – but repairing the damage was going to take about three hours. David suggested we try borrowing guns from a neighbor – but no luck. So David had to rehearse the actors without guns till the locksmith finally rescued the situation. Many other directors would have publicly flayed me for the delay – but he never said a word to anyone, and most of the crew had no idea that anything at all had gone wrong."

What other stories do you have?
"I have so many moments in my head. On **Nine Months**, Chris Columbus chose me to do a scene with Julianne Moore and Hugh Grant – I played a truck

driver for two days. It was fun and I still get residual checks!"

Then on the last year of **Mash**, Bankins shakes his head, "a huge fire broke out at Malibu Ranch, where we were shooting. The assistant directors insisted we finish our schedule that day anyway. The crew thought 'Oh, no!' We evacuated – and a good thing we did. Because when we returned, everything was gone. The sets had burned to the ground, even the metal in the electric cables had melted into the soil.

And I remember on **Young Guns**, sometimes we'd go out to a bar after wrap with Charlie Sheen - that guy was absolutely a babe magnet! Girls always started flirting with him, and then their dates would get mad."

Grumpier Old Men, Bankins recalls, "is full of memories. Walter Mathau never laughed if you told him a joke, but five minutes later, he'd be telling it to someone else, and breaking up. Jack Lemmon was such a sweet human being. He made so little of himself - between takes he'd just sit quietly off in a corner and play with his dog. And Sophia Loren - oh, my! Every morning she'd come and kiss me on each cheek and say 'Hello, Peter'. And I'd dreamed of that woman all through my adolescence!"

What do you enjoy most about the work?

"The job is always new. There are always new problems, things you haven't done before, and you have to invent new solutions. On foreign locations, for instance, you always have to go out and find stuff - and so you get to see unlikely little places and connect with people you wouldn't have met otherwise. It's serious and exciting at the same time!"

SCENIC ARTIST

What does a Scenic Artist do?

"We call ourselves 'liquid magicians' and 'paint wizards', or sometimes 'stunt clown acrobatic speed artists'", says BRIDGET DUFFY, whose credits include **Daddy Daycare** with Eddie Murphy and **Showtime** with Robert De Niro, as well as television's acclaimed **Mad Men.** "We create illusion with paint. We work on all kinds of surfaces, in all kinds of situations and places. We cover props, scenery, and backdrops with a great range of finishes aimed at fooling the eye into seeing what isn't there - not cardboard or canvas, but real wood or marble, a leafy forest, a smoking building, a fiery volcano.

We don't do the designs ourselves, but we carry out – alone or with a crew of as many as twelve, depending on the size of the job - the Art Director's instructions. We climb scaffolds and dangle way high up from lifts. We're gymnasts, we're acrobats, we're contortionists. We squirm into nearly-inaccessible areas high, high above the set - holding onto bucket, paint-brush, spray-gun, or roller with one hand, and working with the other."

What qualifies a Scenic or Graphic Artist?
"Generally, a background in Graphic Arts. I got my B.F.A. from UCLA, and studied further at Los Angeles' Art Center College of Design. I haven't stopped studying since."

How did you begin – get your first job?
Bridget began by painting restaurants. "Then a friend who worked at a television station told me how much better the pay was if you got into the union. The union told me to find work with a union shop for thirty days, and then I could join."

What were some of your more memorable happenings?
"I've yelped at a passerby for help in moving scenery and had Richard Chamberlain rush over and pitch in. Once I was painting scenery next to where Kenny G. was being interviewed, and he planted his foot right in the area where I was working at the exact moment my white brush came down. He ended up with one black shoe and one white! But he was totally nice about it!

Once, at midnight, I was working absolutely alone at Los Angeles' KTTV, painting a playhouse prop for **Different Strokes**. It was a completely soundproof stage, with one-foot-thick doors – when suddenly I saw the entire massive full-length fifteen foot velvet curtain begin to undulate and sway. As if someone were there – but the stage was empty! - I was the only person around and no one had entered or left. The hair on my neck stood on end – I ran! 'Oh yeah', my boss told me casually next morning, 'I forgot to mention the visiting ghost on that stage! We shouldn't have sent you there alone!' He added that numerous crews had reported unexplained sounds and accidents on that stage at night – with no imaginable causes. Gee ... thanks a lot!"

Explain a bit more about "stunt clown acrobatic speed artists".
"I was referring to the insane time frame given to us to produce our work, the impossible positions we have to contort ourselves into in order to reach almost inaccessibly high areas, and the innovative ways we create and invent tools to achieve the unusual paint effects needed to blend our art with actual props. We continue painting during rehearsals of explosions, fight scenes near us, animals charging, fog machines turned on, trap doors revealed, stage lights dimmed, actors running lines, bands cranking up, and dancers kicking their heels inches from us as we rush to finish before the cameras are on us! I've painted many a time with cameras directly over my head or narrowly missing me as I hurried to finish the job. I feel fortunate to have survived for over thirty years in this zany business!"

What do you enjoy about your work?
"I love its amazing variety, artistically and emotionally. Like re-creating Monet's 'Water Lilies', the Mona Lisa, Vermeer's 'Lady With Pearl Earring', Papua-New Guinea Art, Jurassic Age backdrops – and working the Oscars numerous years. Or silly moments like a Japanese reporter asking 'How many buckets of color have you painted today?'

I felt honored to be on stage at the Oscars when Itzhak Perlman and Michael Crawford were rehearsing, or at the American Music Awards when Prince and Cher were working, or hearing Sir Elton John belting it out at CBS. Or being at a CBS fund raiser for New York City the night after 9/11. At that moment I felt that we in entertainment don't merely entertain, but sometimes make a difference in the world.

And then, now and then, from behind the curtain, or back in the wings, I look out and see the joy in people's faces, the laughter, the tears, the whole panorama of human emotions that our efforts evoke. And I love being part of that fabric of life! And thank God for the unions, that stand behind us and maintain the level of respect and financial reward commensurate with our efforts!

But above all, I enjoy the passionate act of applying wet paint to canvas, to muslin, or any surface to create illusion – and will continue to do so until I can no longer hold a brush or see the color of life before me!"

LINDA CASADY, the first woman to become a Scenic Artist, attended Chouinard and Otis Art Schools in Los Angeles, and then began working by painting murals and other decorations on hospital and restaurant walls. Her many eventual film credits would include **All the President's Men, Man on the Moon, Miss Saigon, Phantom of The Opera,** and **Imposter**.

How did you get your first film job?
"Well, I'd heard the pay in television and film was much better than I was earning, and one day I happened to pass through the production area at ABC. I'd

never seen so much paint, such color, huge frames that could go up and down with the push of a button! I was sold. I even asked one of the painters 'D'you really get paid to do this stuff?' He said 'We don't hire women!'"

But Linda "knew I could out-paint and out-draw any man! So I walked into ABC and asked to see the boss who hired Scenic Artists. 'We don't hire women', he repeated, 'but when you're laid off your next job, come back.' Well, one day my sister talked me into going to the races with her - and who do I run into in the Club House but the same boss from ABC. 'My God', he said, 'you followed me to the horse races? You start tomorrow!' After that, I never stopped."

What do you enjoy about the work?
"Every day is an adventure. The biggest stars walk up and want to know what you're doing - Peter Falk, Gregory Peck, Liz Taylor, Julie Andrews.

Once I was standing between Neil Diamond and Warren Beatty, waiting for an elevator from the basement to the set. I was flustered already, and then we got on, and there was Paul Newman! I nearly collapsed! In addition, I was splattered all over with black paint from the work I'd just been doing – and it reminded me of the time my crew had accidentally splashed paint all over Warren's briefcase, his Levis, his shoes. He'd been completely understanding, but still I hoped he didn't remember! Between the three gorgeous guys and the paint, I was so completely rattled I pressed the wrong button and we ended up on the wrong floor.

You learn funny things about people, too - like Michael Jackson changing his clothes at least three or four times a day. And making up different names for himself every time he called you. But he was truly a wonderful person. Once he got to know you, he'd ask lots of questions. One day he said he wished he could draw and paint. I said 'Michael, you're not so bad at what you do!' He laughed."

SPECIAL EFFECTS

What does Special Effects do?

According to DAVE BEAVIS, Special Effects essentially "recreates physical things that can't exist, or can't exist conveniently, on a sound stage - rain, snow, mist – natural elements. And normal things like airplanes and landslides and fires. All to order, in front of the camera".

On **The Conspirator**, for example, Robert Redford's movie about Lincoln's assassination, "we had to make certain items appropriate to the period – such as converting electric lights to gas, and hiding the electrical parts." Computer Generated Images (C.G.I.), on the other hand, "creates things that don't exist at all."

Forty years ago, Beavis says, "we used to do some of what technology does today. But certainly not all of it. The younger directors, brought up on video games, tend to copy films like **Jurassic Park,** with a lot of computer- generated work. Those dinosaurs attacking a jeep couldn't have been created without C.G.I. effects.

All the *Doors* to Hollywood and HOW to *Open* Them

And it would have been impossible to make **Superman** catch a plane in midair."

But often enough, he explains, an effect requires the meeting of Special Effects and Computer Generated Images., as in **Roger Rabbit**. "There, for instance, the C.G.I. cartoon characters interacted with real people – and Special Effects had to create the cartoon characters' shadows, as if they were real. Or, in **Jurassic Park**, they had to create the vehicle the C.G.I. dinosaurs attacked. There's a sort of gray area between the two skills. It can require the best of each.

And Special Effects crews make models and big rigs, "whatever the script calls for. For **Noble House,** for instance, we recreated the large floating restaurants in Hong Kong's Aberdeen Harbor. We have the equipment to do what others can't, like working with heavy metal – steel. Or creating storm waves and whirlpools in water tanks."

What was your background? When did you start in the film business?

"I started when I was fifteen on a movie called **Alfred the Great**." He followed that with David Lean's **Ryan's Daughter,** with Robert Mitchum, John Mills, Trevor Howard and Sarah Miles. "My career beginning", he says, "was kind of a family thing. We lived near Pinewood Studios in London. My mother's father was a carpenter there – my parents actually met in the commissary where my mother worked."

Beavis began at Pinewood as a laborer, "carrying stuff from the truck to the set, and bringing tea and such. I had to gradually learn what I was carrying and why, and how it worked. I had to learn to clean up. By my early twenties, I was doing small effects jobs on my own. By my late twenties, I had my own team."

What skills are needed for your Special Effects crew?
"Well, carpentry and welding, mechanics and electrical know-how – an artistic eye for color and shape and design – a sense of timing – the ability to listen and understand – and basic common sense. You have to be something of a jack-of-all-trades. Willing to take on anything – dirty, dangerous, able to work under the radar. The rest of the set may have no idea what's really going on! And you've got to be able to say 'No' to high-powered directors." A lot of it, he laughs, "is just doing stuff kids like to do – make models, blow things up!"

Where have you worked?
"Everywhere - Africa, Turkey, Switzerland, Macao, Croatia, Hong Kong, Portugal, France, Trinidad –."

What have been some of your favorite adventures?
"I don't know if this is exactly a 'favorite', but what comes first to mind is working on a glacier, in Norway, in the dead of winter, with a blizzard coming on, for the movie **Gulag.** There was just blue ice, no snow yet". The problem was that Beavis had to help get the crew off the ice as soon as possible – but there were more people than vehicles to carry them. "We soon couldn't see a thing – not even our trucks and deep track vehicles. We got some crew down, and then had to go back up for the rest in full blizzard conditions. We made it - but it was a lucky escape."

Some favorite people you've worked with?

"Robert Redford's certainly one of them. The man's really on his game. He knows what he wants, and at the same time, he lets his people do their thing. He inspires confidence in his actors and crew."

What do you enjoy about your work?

"It's great to agree up front with the production on your price, have them pretty much hand you a wad of money and hear them say 'We'll meet back here in three months'. In other words,' Go and do your thing'. And then there's that first moment, the mystery, when you've gotten the job and look at what it entails – it's a thrill moment. You think 'I've never done this before'. And then comes the challenge, the figuring it out. And you know the very first time you'll actually find out if you've really solved it will be the critical moment in front of the camera! I guess that's true of every film department. But every time, it's really something!"

TRANSPORTATION

What does a Transportation Coordinator do on a movie?

"A lot of things. A lot", says JIM THORNSBERRY, who estimates he's done "at least fifty" movies and television series. The first thing I do when I'm hired, is break the script down - how long the projected schedule is, whether there are night shoots, whether there are one or more locations and where, whether there are animals, children –. Endless details."

Children? What difference does having children make?

"Kids have to find schoolrooms on location, I have to provide chairs, desks –."

And then?

"I find out who the director is - that can make a huge difference. Sam Peckinpah, for example, Robert Altman - very expensive, spare no cost - they want all the drivers available at all times. That kind of thing affects

All the *Doors* to Hollywood and HOW to *Open* Them

the budget. Then I find out where we're going to film, the terrain - whether there are night shoots, whether there are dogs, other animals - special provisions have to be made. I find out whether we're doing 'off road' or 'on road' locations. 'Off road' means things like desert areas, mountains. I'm in charge of the generators, the cranes, the trailers for the actors, for Props and Make-up and Costume – all that. And I have to get the vehicles to wherever we're going - the honeywagons, too - the portable restrooms for everyone. There are always special considerations. Desert shoots require particular kinds of vehicles that can navigate the sand. And we'll need water trucks."

And after all that?
"With all that information, I'll do a preliminary budget and compare it with the film's projected budget - the amount assigned my department. And make adjustments. Then I get my standing crew together - five people in addition to myself is a minimum. On location, we pick up local drivers, if necessary."

How did you get started?
"I began at twenty-one or twenty-two. My father was in the business, in transportation, and my Aunt Irene was head of the Nurse's Union. I'd been in the Navy - I joined with Johnny Weismuller, Jr., who was my dearest friend, and with Ryan O'Neill. I had about two years in the Navy, went to Santa Monica City College, had some odd jobs like Greensman at Fox Studios, and then got into the transportation department there. I started working as a driver on movies - for a while I owned a

limousine company and rented out honeywagons to the studios - restrooms and dressing rooms. And from there I talked myself into being a Transportation Captain - we call it Coordinator, now. And that's where I've been ever since."

What are some of the movies you've done and the actors you've worked with?
"More than I can probably remember. **The Game** with Michael Douglas, **Virtuosity** with Denzel Washington, **Sliver** with Sharon Stone, **Patriot Games** with Harrison Ford, **Class Action** with Gene Hackman, **Marrying Man** with Alec Baldwin and Kim Basinger, **Dead Again** with Kenneth Branagh, Emma Thompson, and Robin Williams, **Winter People** with Kurt Russell and Kelly McGillis –. And then there are the older movies like **Getaway** with Steve McQueen and Ali McGraw, and **Shampoo** with Warren Beatty and Julie Christie. I did **F.I.S.T.** with Sylvester Stallone - that was the Jimmy Hoffa story."

Do foreign locations present special problems?
"Special considerations, again. On **Clear and Present Danger,** shot in Mexico with Harrison Ford and Ann Archer, we had to negotiate Customs, figure out what we could take through and how to do it. If the movie's going to have a Second Unit, that means additional equipment."

Who've been some of your favorite people?
"I've met some of the best people in the world. There's the director, Robert Weiss – they don't come

any better than that. And Harrison Ford – just a great guy. A humane, caring person. The producer Charlie McGuire was as good as they come. And Steve McQueen, Kenneth Branagh, Emma Thompson –."

What do you enjoy about the work?
"We have to deal with absolutely everybody in the entire movie, so it's always interesting, always new. We're not limited to any special area – we're the basic support system for the entire production. And the challenges - the problems to be solved, the people, the locations that are always changing. We see so much of the world. It couldn't be a better job."

GRAPHIC DESIGN

What is the Graphic Designer's job?

"We do all the signs and graphics on a movie", says LILLIAN HEYWARD. "We paint, we draw, we design. On **Force of Nature**, for instance, with Ben Affleck and Sandra Bullock, we did the airplane logo, the plane's seat numbers, the signs on the bus, on the taxis and trains, the bagel shop –."

Graphic Designers are responsible for any print or facsimile of print that is needed. And often, as in the Civil War period film **The Conspirator,** research is necessary to determine and accurately reproduce the era's print and cursive styles. "A sign can help set the mood of the scene – is it slightly crooked and weather beaten, with clearly hand-done fonts, for a run-down junkyard? Is it slick and ultra-modern for corporate headquarters? Is it slightly bent and ominous with out-dated fonts for a deserted shipyard where a murder will take place?"

What background prepared you for this work?

Lillian began studying illustration, and then switched to graphic design, first at Maine College of Art in Portland, and then at the Philadelphia College of Art. "Then I had a patchwork of jobs -. I fell in love with a Swede and spent some time in Sweden as an assistant art teacher in a middle school and after that working for a sign company. Next came Gibraltar and a sign company again, this time designing fonts, and after that back to the States and a sign company in Hilton Head, South Carolina."

For a time Lillian worked as a shrimper on a shrimp boat - and with the money saved from that, she opened her own sign and graphic design shop in Beaufort, South Carolina. "We did signage and brochures for a real estate company development, 'way-finding' signs for a hospital - you know, directional help. And we even did signs for the county jail - so help me, it was actually a color coordinated jail! My first experience with film was subcontracting for **Prince of Tides,** with Barbara Streisand. Then in 1991 my sign shop burned and I was devastated, but then I realized I had a skill I could use on movies."

Heyward's first full film job was the Coen Brothers' **Hudsucker Proxy** with Paul Newman and Tim Robbins. "A friend on the film, Sandy Dawes, got me an interview in Wilmington North Carolina. That's the one", she says, "where I had to build the Brooklyn Bridge – a model, anyway. It was a strange request. With the Art Director and lead painter, we created the bridge, which appears in the opening scene. We made it in ten minutes, literally - it was only a model. But I had stars in my eyes!

I loved the challenge, the creativity, and the pressure to solve problems - quickly! I fell in love with movies!

After I returned home to Beaufort, I got a call from the art director. The people I'd worked with on **Hudsucker** were coming to Beaufort. So my second movie as sign writer was **Forrest Gump.**"

What movies have been among your favorites to have worked on?

"Lasse Hallstrom's **Dear John** and Robert Redford's **The Conspirator,** of course. And **Big Mama Like Father Like Son.** The movies you love are always about the people you work with and not necessarily how big the box office will be. It's like any job in life, when you get to work with the people you like and respect, nothing is better."

What have been some memorable moments?

"On **Dear John**, I was told 'You've twenty minutes to find the logo of the Romanian TV station that broadcast the attack on the World Trade Center!' I got lucky. I not only found it, but the footage of the attack as well - with about two seconds to go! Although being faced with seeing that scene again was chilling."

And then, Lillian says, research for **The Conspirator** was fascinating. The movie covers the treason trial of Mary Surrat, who owned the boarding house where Abraham Lincoln's killer, John Wilkes Booth, stayed. "I had to comb the Library of Congress to find written material of the period, *carte de visites* and specific documents – the trial transcript, the writ of habeas corpus - the plea for clemency for Surrat. The plea, written in the florid cursive of the period, was practically indecipherable. If the judges at the time had as much trouble reading it as I did – no wonder Mary Surrat was the first woman to be hanged in this country!"

What do you enjoy about your work?

"It's never monotonous! You design, you paint, you get to use all your skills, and think on your feet - sometimes I use my own paintings – you draw, you research. You learn stuff. When you contract to a job, you never really know what you're going to get. I love what I do!"

SET DECORATOR

What does a Set Decorator do?

"Well", says Set Decorator TRICIA SCHNEIDER, "it's sort of like a perpetual scavenger hunt. I discuss with the Director and the Production Designer all the things that will add to the script, or fill in the blank spots - all the between-the-lines elements. Objects that add dimension to the character or the scene - furniture, carpets, drapes, washing machines, radios, books - whatever might show how the character lives or has chosen to live, or the situation he or she is currently in. The mood, the era –. The script doesn't tell you everything.

I start by breaking the script down into sets, and what's happening in each, whether it's period or not, what era, and what I need. Then, if called for, I research the particular period, I look at old photos or paintings, I look in costume books –. In the movie **All the King's Men,** with Sean Penn and Jude Law, I needed a 'forties drug store with a soda fountain, a counter, and stools. Another time, I needed to do a strip club for the movie **Ice Harvest.** I went to a lot of them, I looked at personal photos people had taken. I'm a kind of detective."

How did you get started?
"I got a Bachelor of Fine Arts Degree and then spent several years as studio manager for a still photographer. From there I managed to move into commercials, as an Art Director – I did Nascar commercials for which I had to create an authentic Nascar garage, and worked for Dow Chemical on a commercial about desalinization. I had to learn all about the process. From there I moved into features as a Set Decorator. A film producer I knew from my work in commercials believed in me."

What was your first feature?
"**Kissing Fool,** with Jason Leigh and David Schwimmer, was my first movie. I've done **Hardball** with Keanu Reeves and Diane Lane, **Ali** with Will Smith, **Barbershop One** with Ice Cube, **Normal** with Jessica Lange and Tom Wilkinson. **Ice Harvest** had a terrific pair, Billy Bob Thornton and John Cusack –."

Any foreign locations?
"Aruba and Tortola in the Caribbean, Mexico –."

What actors have you particularly liked?
"Actually, I've enjoyed all of them. Diane Lane, for instance, John Cusack, Billy Bob Thornton, Sean Penn - I've never had a bad experience."

ANNE M. STRICK

What are the some of the weirdest things you've had to find, and some of the craziest experiences you've had?

"I think the weirdest thing I've had to find, so far, was a set of matching stained urinals for the movie **Ice Harvest**, the one with John Cusack and Billy Bob Thornton. They needed to be not only stained, but cracked – which only comes with time. We searched all over junk yards for them - found them finally in a place complete with the junk yard dog that bites, and the rats, and the grimy old owner in his falling-down shack with a sheet covering the holes in his floor. Another time we had to find an entire 'forties amusement park - merry-go-round, Ferris wheel, all of it. We looked all over the country for that one. And there've been an iron lung - it was heavy as a Volks-wagen - surveillance vehicles, appliances of just about all kinds, from a range of eras.

One of the times that was most fun was on **Ice Harvest**, hanging Christmas lights and decorations along an entire set of streets in Waukegan, Illinois. We were all singing carols and laughing - it was awesome! I think 'insanity day' was the time five different five-ton trucks went off in five different directions with set dressings we'd needed absolutely right away. And then there's the ridiculous memory of my Swing Gang running around catching huge rats in the warehouse we were working in - the darn rats had been eating up all our animal crackers! And then there was the Director who kept repainting the set literally every day - getting paint on all the equipment, and all our clothes –."

What is a Swing Gang?

"My crew. Another name is 'Set Dressers'. They go in before we set up anywhere - make sure everything I want gets to its appointed place, and pick it up afterwards. There's a permanent 'Lead Man', and the minimum crew is five people. It can go up to twenty, depending on the situation. We often pick up the additional ones in each new city."

Where do you look for all the strange items you need?

"Everywhere. Antique shops, junk yards, flea markets, retail stores, the Internet and E-Bay - and we ask people."

What do you enjoy most about what you do?

"I love observing people. Even in Laundromats. I love hand-painted signs, and all the things in peoples' old junk drawers - they tell you who the person is. I love creating beyond the script. A lot of it will never be seen on screen, in fact, but it creates an environment for the actor that fills out the character. I love the enormous variety of people I meet - the hours just fly by. I met my husband on **Save the Last Dance!**"

COSTUME DESIGNER

How does a costume designer go about the job?

"It's all very precise", says LOUISE FROGLEY, among whose credits are **The Conspirator** and **Men Who Stare at Goats,** and who has been in the business for thirty-five years.

"First, I'm sent the script, and then, if I haven't worked with these people before, there's an interview – and then, if it's a good fit, I'm hired. At that point, I hire a Supervisor, who understands costumers – perhaps with a background in uniforms, - and all that needs to be done – keeps track of the materials and the personnel. I break the script down into characters, and what they'll wear, and do designs and a budget. I get the director's approval of the designs. Trucks are hired – separate ones for the principals' and the extras' costumes - with great care that nothing gets lost or misplaced. For instance, there are muslins on which smaller items, like jewelry, are pinned, and boxes for things like shoes and purses and hats - all marked."

Next, Louise says, comes fittings. "We photograph it all, so we have a record of exactly what was discussed with the actor, and with the seamstress, and what alterations will be made. We show the footage to the director – some of them come to fittings, some don't."

How do Costume and Wardrobe differ?
"Wardrobe is the support system for Costume. It covers the shoppers, the fitters, the sewers."

What was your background for this work?
"I went to Hornsey College of Art in London for five years – took every course they had. I've always loved textiles. I began by working for a photographer, doing set dressing but getting paid very little. Finally, I offered to do his designing. One of my first jobs was putting together a stately home to be photographed, complete with staff, location, even tea! I gradually assembled a presentation book with my work displayed, and with it got my first television commercials.

Eventually I did loads of commercials – Pepsi, Nike - and one of those directors gave me my first film job."

Where have you worked?
"Hong Kong, China, Morocco, Atlanta, Savannah, Detroit, Casablanca –."

Which have been among your favorite directors, and films?
"Among directors, Steven Soderbergh and George Clooney. The movies that come to mind are **Traffic, The Good German, Ocean's 13, Syriana, Ides of March, Men Who Stare at Goats, Limey, The Conspirator.**"

And your favorite actors?
"Jeff Bridges, most certainly. And George Clooney, Robin Wright, Rachel Weiss –."

What do you like most about these particular people, directors and actors?
"Their boundless enthusiasm, their energy, and their commitment to detail and character. They're terrific to work with!"

Filming adventures?
"There is sometimes cultural confusion. Perhaps the funniest was on **Syriana**. We shot in Morocco, and we always seemed to be presented with the wrong Arabs for the one Arab country of the movie - Palestinians, Saudis, Lebanese – each group of extras turning up with slightly different accessories, headgear –. We had to take extra precaution, so that by filming they'd all be dressed alike.

And in China, they'd always be agreeable, and then not follow through as promised. Politeness seems primary. And they'd wear anything, whatever the scene to be filmed, so finally we realized we had to dress them ourselves. And then when we wanted the ethnic group called Hakka to wear their traditional hats, they just wouldn't. We never understood why."

What do you enjoy about the work?
"The puzzle. There's always something to solve. And I like choosing things – textiles, colors, shapes. And navigating between actors' and directors' preferences. And, of course the travel! I can't wait to go again!"

MAKE-UP

What is it like to be a Make-Up Artist? What do you do?

"I love it", says BEVERLY JO PRYOR, who suspects she's made up "over a thousand people" by now. "In a way, we're sort of therapists. We make sure the actors look the part, of course, we find out what the Director wants. But we also try to make the actors happy - confident - so they'll do their best."

How do you go about it?

Beverly Jo begins by talking with the Director and the actor to find out how they see the actor's character. "I like to make the actors part of their look, because then they'll feel better about themselves." Next, she does whatever research may be required - is it a contemporary or period film, a science fiction movie or, perhaps, adventure. She breaks the script down - "are there going to be special effects, is there going to be blood, sweating, crying, kissing. Special make-up is applied in each case. "Maybe there are even teeth braces for the kids!"

Then "I want to be sure my Make-Up trailer has a soothing feeling." She selects relaxing music and a soft, pleasant aroma, she lights candles and places crystals on a small altar, "all to create positive energy and set the right mood. I pay attention to whether the actor wants to talk, or wants silence. I listen to them, I tell them how great they look - if they feel good about themselves, it helps them do their best."

Beverly Jo keeps a continuity book, taking photos as the script requires the actor's look to change, "so that if maybe old scenes have to be re-shot, I'll know what to do." She notes everything she does and uses. "And there's a special make-up bag for each actor, with his or her name on it, and a photo - so I - or someone else - can just grab the right bag and go."

How did you get started?

"I'd wanted to be a dancer, or a choreographer or an actress. Or a painter. But I got married right out of high school, and had kids right away - and I wanted to be the best Mom possible. My background was creative. My father was a clothes designer and tailor and taught at a technical school. He very much wanted to own his own shop, but he was black - and in Topeka, Kansas, in the 'forties, a black man couldn't open his own business. So we moved to Denver, and he got a job in the Post Office - a middle class position for a black man in those days. But he continued to make clothes for me, and I modeled them."

Her marriage broke up, "and I was a single mom, and needed part-time work. I did a number of things, and then I got a job with Max Factor Cosmetics as a 'beauty consultant' after a one-time training program." Beverly Jo had always loved to paint. "I thought, gosh, this is great! I'm doing what I love, and getting paid for it!"

Beverly Jo's brother's best friend was a photographer. "I began doing make-up for his subjects - head shots - and gradually built up a portfolio." Meanwhile, continuing to do make-up on the side, she finished raising her children; at the same time managing part-time jobs as a Customer Representative for America West Airlines, working as a legal secretary, and attending California State University at Long Beach.

When did you actually begin doing movies?
"I started with commercials. Then television and Award Shows, and then I moved into features. My first was **Mo Money.** Both **Ali** with Will Smith and **Posse** with Mario and Melvin Van Peebles were a lot of fun. I've worked with some great people - Nona Gay, Marvin's daughter, and Pam Grier, Michel Jordan, Milton Berle, Debbie Allen, Tyra Banks, John Candy, Quincy Jones - and the list goes on. I treat everyone as special - first-time actor, or a star, or an old friend."

Where have you done films?
"I've worked all over the United States and Canada, the Caribbean, South Africa –."

What was your favorite adventure?
Probably going on Safari in South Africa - Kruger Park, while we were filming **Ali.** It's a huge wild animal preserve - jungle and bush and big open plains - and I

think I saw just about every kind of wild animal there is. Rhinos and antelope, buffalo, giraffes, wildebeest, lions, leopards, hyenas, crocodiles. Everything except zebras. And I'd never seen so many kinds of birds. It was all just wonderful."

What do you enjoy about your work?
"I love doing my art and getting immediate results. And I'm a 'people person', and there are always new ones to get to know as well as old familiars. I'm always meeting new people. I love the irregularity of the work, too. Not only the irregular schedule of the days, but having new jobs in new places all the time. I love, maybe most of all, that it's a team effort - cooperative - all of us working towards one goal. I thank God every day that I can do what I love and make a living!"

PUBLICIST

What does a movie publicist do?

"A lot of things", says publicist LEONARD MORPURGO. "Basically, I blow the film's horn. As a Unit Publicist, I bring television and print media to the set. I get photos of the movie's stars in magazines and newspapers, get stories about them on television, blogs, Facebook, and Twitter. As the print world disappears, these outlets become increasingly important. I soothe nervous actors, calm bristly egos, buffer the often competing interests and suspicions of stars, directors, producers, and studios. And I write."

What do you write?

"I do press releases, biographies of the stars, the director, the producer, for the press-kit - and a synopsis of the movie's plot, all so that journalists and critics have a background for their articles. And I record for the ages those gossipy bits that everyone loves - those that are publishable!" The work is intense, exhausting, and very frequently a great deal of fun. "The publicist has a ringside seat at most of the aspects of movie-making and promoting, as well as an upfront look at all the personalities and dramas involved." Travel to far-off locations is often part of the job "and there, you really see the stars up close!"

What qualifies the publicist?

"A degree and/or experience in journalism, communications, or marketing helps. But the publicist may be simply a literate human being with imagination, drive, and a significant degree of organization and diplomatic skills."

The Studio Publicist, Morpurgo explains, "unlike the free-lance Unit Publicist who works film to film, is a full-time studio employee." Among other duties, the Studio Publicist sets up film-screenings for press and television reporters, creates web-sites for films, and corrals those all-important celebrities to appear at premieres. "Which of course further publicizes both the movie and the celebrity."

Who are some of these publicists, how did they start, and what stories do they tell?

Leonard Morpurgo began his career as a journalist in England, and soon landed a job as a press release writer for a British film distribution company. "I was promoted to 'press officer' (publicity director) after my boss was found lying in a drunken stupor on his living room floor. Since then, I've had a close-up seat at all kinds of small dramas and comedies.

ANNE M. STRICK

Once I was working as a Unit Publicist on a movie starring Gene Hackman and another well-known actor - **Target**. The two stars didn't get on too well. After four months shooting in Paris, Hamburg, and Corpus Christi, Texas, I'd still failed to get the two men grinning chummily together for the obligatory 'best buddies' photo. It was near wrap. I had only two days left. I was desperate.

'How can I do it?'" Hackman demanded. "'I don't like him!'

'Gene, you're an actor. A great actor. *Act.*'"

They got the shot.

Then there was the movie **Leaving Las Vegas** with Nicholas Cage. "Cage portrayed an alcoholic - he actually had a 'drinking coach' to teach him how! Nicholas was doing magnificently until, for a climactic scene, his coach insisted he hang one on for real. Cage agreed. From the moment he got out of bed the next morning until the start of shooting that afternoon, he drank. On the first scene, a dash through a Casino, he knocked over a waitress. He was supposed to do that. In the second scene, he knocked over a blackjack table, broke it, and cut his hand. He was not supposed to do that! But it hadn't been a total loss. That was the movie he got an Oscar for!"

CAROL GREEN *has a ream of stories.*

"In my twenty-plus years on set", Carol laughs, "I've dealt with some not so 'press worthy' situations where quick thinking was necessary to avoid embarrassment and minimize damage. These are often hilarious – but only in the aftermath of sheer panic!"

All the *Doors* to Hollywood and HOW to *Open* Them

For example?

"Well – one time, while waltzing an important journalist through the set of a major television production, I spotted our seriously agitated lead actor smash his fist into a wall with such power that he actually broke his hand! While the paramedics rushed in behind us, I managed to pull our guest into an adjacent rose garden, praising the talent of our Greens Department so loudly that the reporter missed all the off-screen-on-set drama, - which would have made a great cover story for her - but definitely not for us."

Then, Carol laughs, "there was the time shooting in Miami Beach when two actors lost it. They just lost it. Hate had been brewing since day one. By the time **Access Hollywood** arrived on set, the two were at full throttle, *mano a mano*, in a fistfight. The crew's drivers jumped in to break it up – while I quickly herded the **Access** group to a down-the-street espresso bar where I vigorously extolled the delights of late afternoon iced latte.

Meanwhile, back on the set, as one of the actors climbed into the van headed to the hospital for post-altercation repair, he managed to add injury to injury by clipping himself on the forehead as he whipped open the van door. Another couple of stitches! Not good. But **Access** missed it all. And the lattes", she laughs, "were great. My treat."

These are war stories!

"Here's another", Carol says, "a personal favorite. It involves Jack Nicholson. We were shooting **Blood and Wine** at a private home in Miami Beach where the expensive mansion was just perfect for our needs - including a well-appointed yacht docked out back. On the first day of production, about forty-five minutes before we were to get our first shot, I got a 911 from a very nervous executive producer.

Seems that although the set was plastered with warning signs to respect the residents' privacy and not leave the clearly demarked set area, some unknown person had violated this strict policy. The owners were up in arms, threatening to shut down production. I was recruited to save the day - placate the residents and convince them not to kick us out. Because if we lost this location, a new location would have been far too costly for our budget. The whole film would have gone down in flames.

After conferring with the producer to get the full skinny on things, I was ushered into the den where the distraught homeowner and his decidedly younger Puerto Rican trophy wife were just this side of hysterical. Nevertheless he managed to offer me a seven a.m. scotch - while his wife collapsed across the couch sobbing quietly - intermittently mopping her tears on the fur of a miniscule Chihuahua draped around her neck.

'Oh dear. What's the matter?

'Ralph Lauren is dead.'

'Ralph Lauren is *dead?*'

'*Si. Dio mio*', she sobbed.

I was shocked. What a talented man, I thought, and so young!

"In actuality", Carol explains, "the tragedy had nothing to do with the famous fashion designer at all. Turns out, the lady of the house owned five Chihuahuas - all named after iconic designers: Valentino, Coco Chanel, Armani, Versace, and the just dearly-departed Ralph Lauren. Topping that, however, was the unfortunate little incident I'd been called in to handle. It seems the mourning wife was resting in the nude when someone from our production blundered into her boudoir unannounced. She was mortified; her husband was enraged."

Carol began her investigation. As luck would have it, the intruder was none other than Jack Nicholson himself.

"Oh, happy day! Offering the company's condolences for the loss of Ralph and our apologies for the lady's embarrassment in her bedroom, we pointed out our star's reputation as a world famous connoisseur of beautiful women. After all, who better than Jack to appreciate a body so gorgeous it needed no clothes? Her husband was indeed a very lucky man!"

Make note, Carol directs. "Flattery is a great tool in a circumstance like this. Over the next week, we bundled that line together with a hand-in-hand awed tour of the glitzy house by Jack and the lady in question, a reverent visit to Ralph's final resting place, and a glamorous role for Madame as an extra in the yacht scene – all interwoven with the reminder that the couple could dine out on the story for the rest of their lives." As a result, the production was finally given permission to remain. "It's one of those odd little behind-the-scenes events you never hear about", Carol reminds, but "don't you wish you did?

POSTSCRIPT

There are, of course, many more doors to Hollywood than the foregoing. There other behind-the-scenes wizards - wizards who make the magic happen - than these. There are, for instance, assistant directors, crafts service people, cameramen, hair stylists, plasterers, wardrobe personnel, production managers and coordinators, production assistants, mechanics, painters, sculptors, nurses, teachers, caterers, and many more.

A list of all of these additional people, and of the IATSE guilds and locals that represent them, will be found on the two next pages; with contact data.

See this list for possible follow-up information to this book: for IATSE membership requirements, and possible employment opportunities.

Meanwhile, good luck. And look forward to *All The Doors to Hollywood and How to Open Them, Volume Two.*

All the *Doors* to Hollywood and HOW to *Open* Them

THE FOLLOWING IATSE GUILDS AND LOCALS WILL SUPPLY UP-TO-DATE MEMBERSHIP AND EMPLPOYMENT INFORMATION. THEIR PHONE NUMBERS, WEBSSITES AND EMAIL ADDRESSES ARE LISTED FOR POSSIBLE QUERIES.

Local	Craft	Phone Number	Email and website
33	Stage Hands, Theatrical employees, Theater Property Master	818-769-2500	Local33@IATSE33.com www.IA33.org
44	Carpenters, Props/ Special, Visual Effects, Food Stylists, Construction Moving Picture Property Master, Set Decorators, Set Dressers, Props, Landscaping/ Greensman	818-769-2500	callboard@local44.org www.local44.org
80	Grips, Craft Services, Rigging Grips	818-526-0700	Solidarity80@hotmail.com www.IATSElocal80.org
600	D.P.Director of Photography, Camera Photography, Publicists Guild	323-876-0160	Dave.tweDell.com www.cameraguild.com
695	Foley, Sound Technicians, Projectionists, Sound Editors, VTR	818-985-9204	695@695.com www.local695.com
700	Editors, Studio Projectionists, Story Analysts, Film Tech., Negative Cutters	323-876-4770	www.editorsguild.com
705	Costumers, MP	818-487-5655	MPC705@AOLK.com www.motionpicture costumers.org
706	Hair Stylists, Make-Up Artists	818-295-3933	info@IAlocal706.org www.local706.org

Local	Craft	Phone Number	Email and website
707	Mixed Crafts (carpentry, audio, props, wardrobe, electriaal)	760-3340-6323	IATSElocal707@veerizon.net
728	Electricians, Gaffers	818-985-0728	Loc728@IATSE728.org www.IATSE728.org
729	Set Painters, Sign Writers	818-842-7729	George@Ialocal729.com www.IAlocal729.com
755	Sculptors, Modelers, Plasterers	818-379-9985	www.local755.com
767	First Aid, Medical Employees	818-842-7670	sectreasurer@IATSE.org www.IATSE767.org
768	Wardrobe, Theatrical	818-843-8768	Wardrobe768@yahoo.com
800	Production Designers, Art Directors, Scenic Artists, Title Artists, Storyboard Artists, Credits Artists, Graphic Artists, Matte Artists, Illustrators, Set Designers, Model Makers	818-762-9995	Lydia@artdirectors.org www.artdirectors.org
839	Animation, Cartoonists, Visual Effects	818-845-7500	infor@animationguild.org www.animationguild.org
871	Accountants, Prod. Office Coordinator &Accountants, Script Supervisor & Continuity, Teleprompter	818-509-7871	missy@IAlocal871.org www.IAlocal871.org
884	Teachers, Studio	310-652-5330	www.studioteachers.com pollyfuisse@aol.com
892	Costume Designers Guild	818-752-2400	cdgIA@costumedesginersguild.com www.costumedesignersguild.com

Other Books by Anne M. Strick

OTHER BOOKS
BY ANNE M. STRICK
(Available wherever books are sold)

THE REBEL PRINCESS
The behind-the-scenes skinny on the secrets of a film company on location in Mexico, this intense novel follows the making of a movie, in an exotic world, from preproduction through wrap.

*"Anne M. Strick's THE REBEL PRINCES is a revealing insider's scoop on how movies are **really** made – gritty, grinding, tunnel-vision labor, backstage intrigue, explosive dramas, parties and relationships that can either last a night of a lifetime. It rang so true and I had such a blast, I couldn't put it down!"*
Raffaella De Laurentiis
Producer
Raffaella Productions

INTIMATE STRANGERS
Intimate Strangers is the rich, complex and passionate story of a contested adoption and the two women who join to save small boy's life. The book examines the various faces of love: erotic love and romantic love, the love of parent for child and child for parent; and what "really" makes a parent.

All the *Doors* to Hollywood and HOW to *Open* Them

The book's suspenseful focus is on the child's fate - and on the relationship between the women, law partners with widely divergent and equally traumatic histories; who battle on his behalf. The case strikes at the heart of each. Out of their own shadowy backgrounds, the women make a stunning discovery – and must decide what to do about it, and what to do about the men in their lives.

This is a story of loss, of healing and redemption. And at the same time, a heartfelt plea for justice in our courts for the most helpless among us.

"This wonderful book is the first to focus on one aspect of man's inhumanity to child that has crossed my path many times: that confusing world of adoptions. Anne M. Srick artfully sets up parallel adoption scenarios that immerse the reader in the very hearts of the characters – birth parents, adoptive parents, and, most importantly, the hearts of the children themselves. With this book, she gives us the impetus to legally, practically and morally move to fulfill for our children the promise of the Pledge of Allegiance – 'With Liberty and Justice for All'".

Judge Charles D. Gill
Connecticut Superior Court Judge
Board Member of First Star

INJUSTICE FOR ALL
(Available on Amazon)

This heretical and visionary non-fiction book explains why our adversary trial system not only does not – but cannot - deliver the justice it promises. And offers, for discussion and experiment, an alternative path to that goal: a legal system in which information, rather than winning, is paramount.

"This original and arresting work raises troubling questions about our whole theory of the way to justice. It deserves wide and thoughtful reading."
Arthur Schlesinger, Jr.
Ptulitzer Prize-winning historian,
Schweitzer Professor of Humanities,
City University of New York

"Personally, I do not agree with Ms. Strick's criticisms or recommendations. But Injustice For All may prove a catalyst for the modulation of the system............Perhaps Injustice For All may unwittingly become a judicial innovator, rousing the public as well as the lawyers to action and thus initiate a second renaissance in judicial administration."
Tom C. Clark,
former Justice, U.S. Supreme Court

CPSIA information can be obtained at www.ICGtesting.com
Printed in the USA
LVOW102231040313

322698LV00013B/178/P

9 781477 569153